DINOSAUR
COLORING BOOK

Dinosaurs
Coloring Book for Kids

Dinosaur
Colouring Pages

COOL2BKIDS.COM

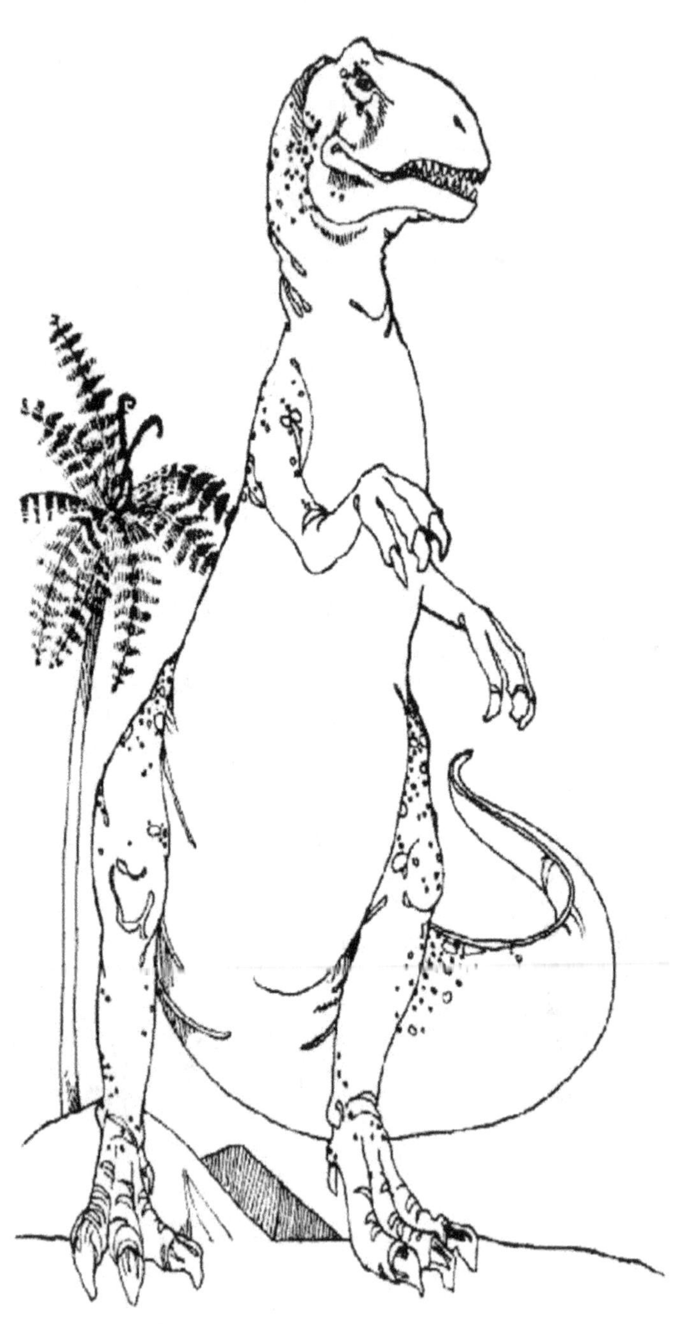

coloringfree.blogspot.com

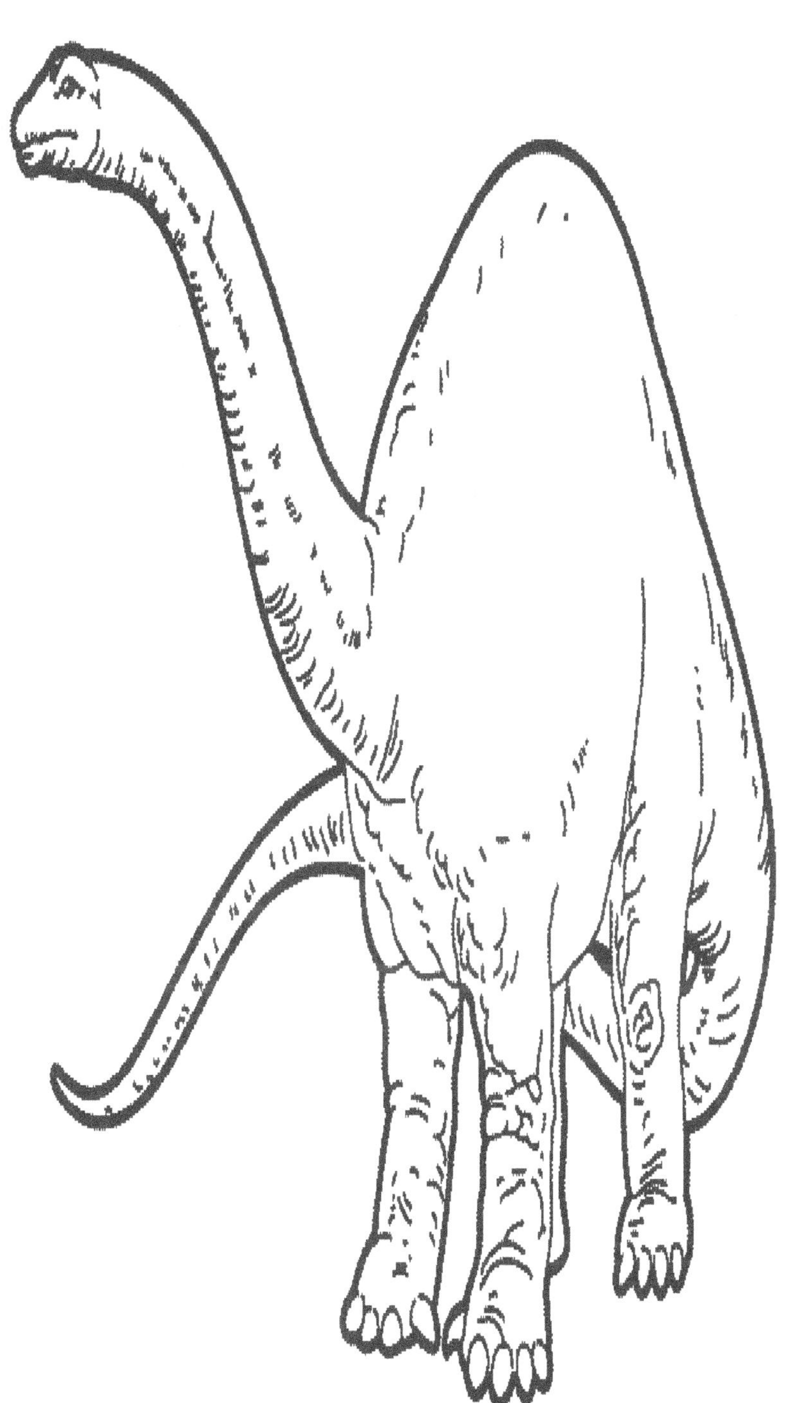

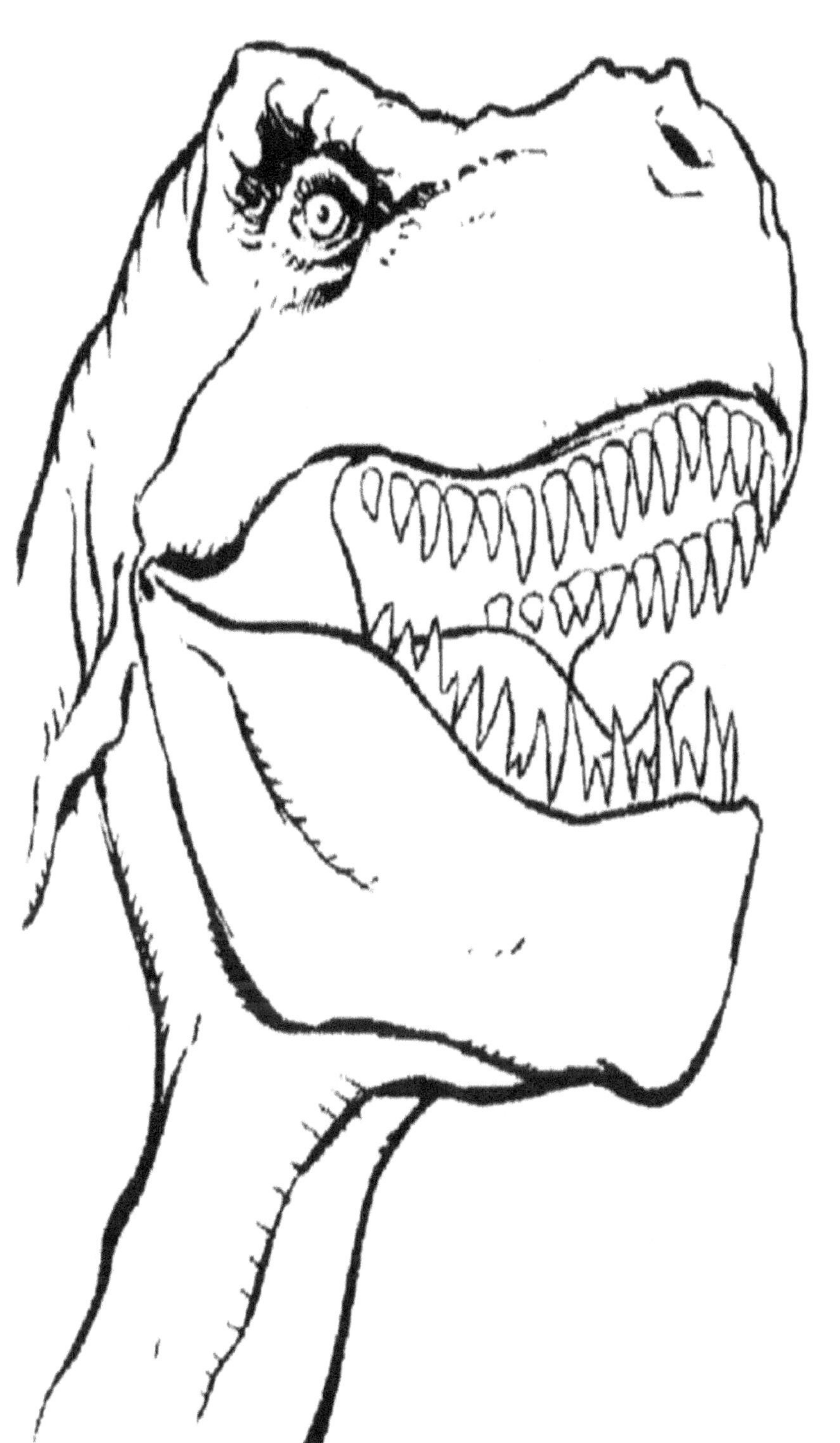

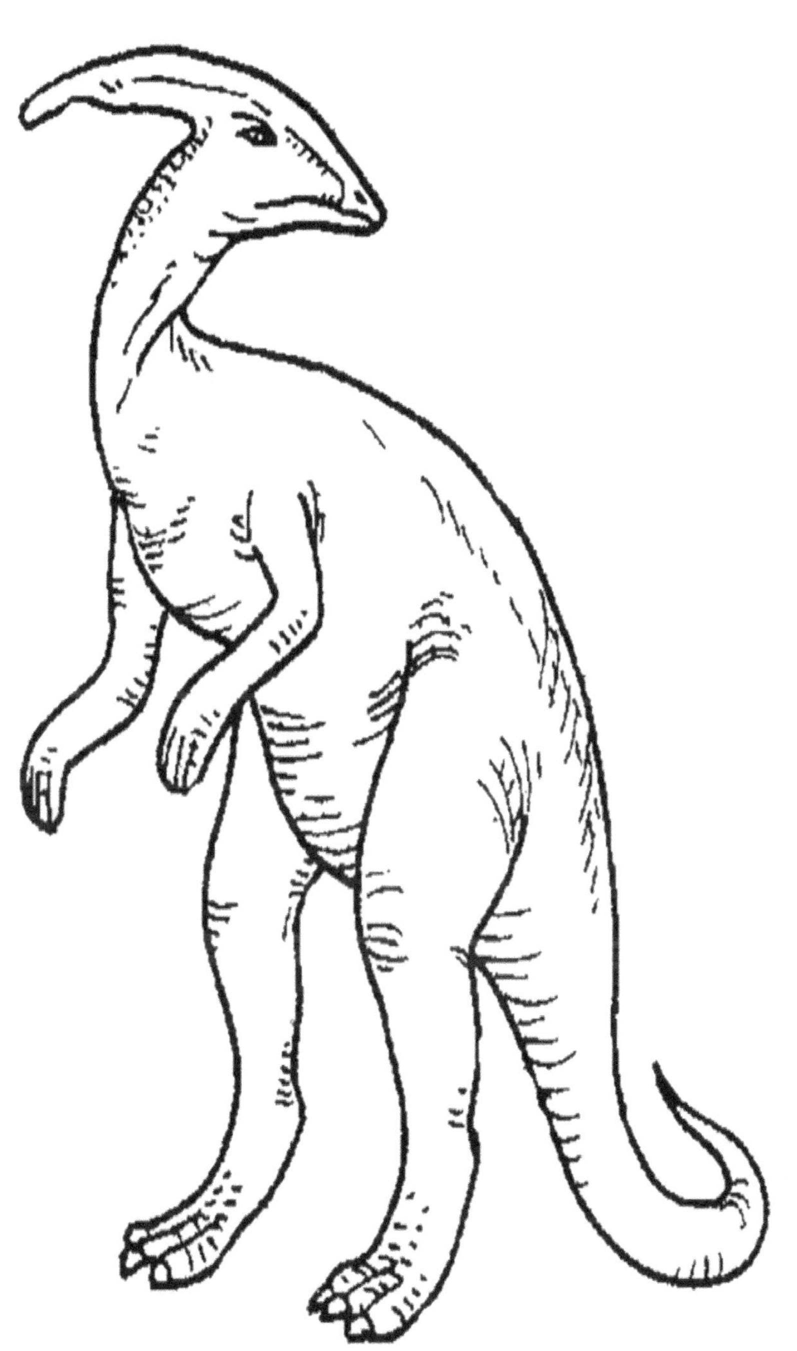

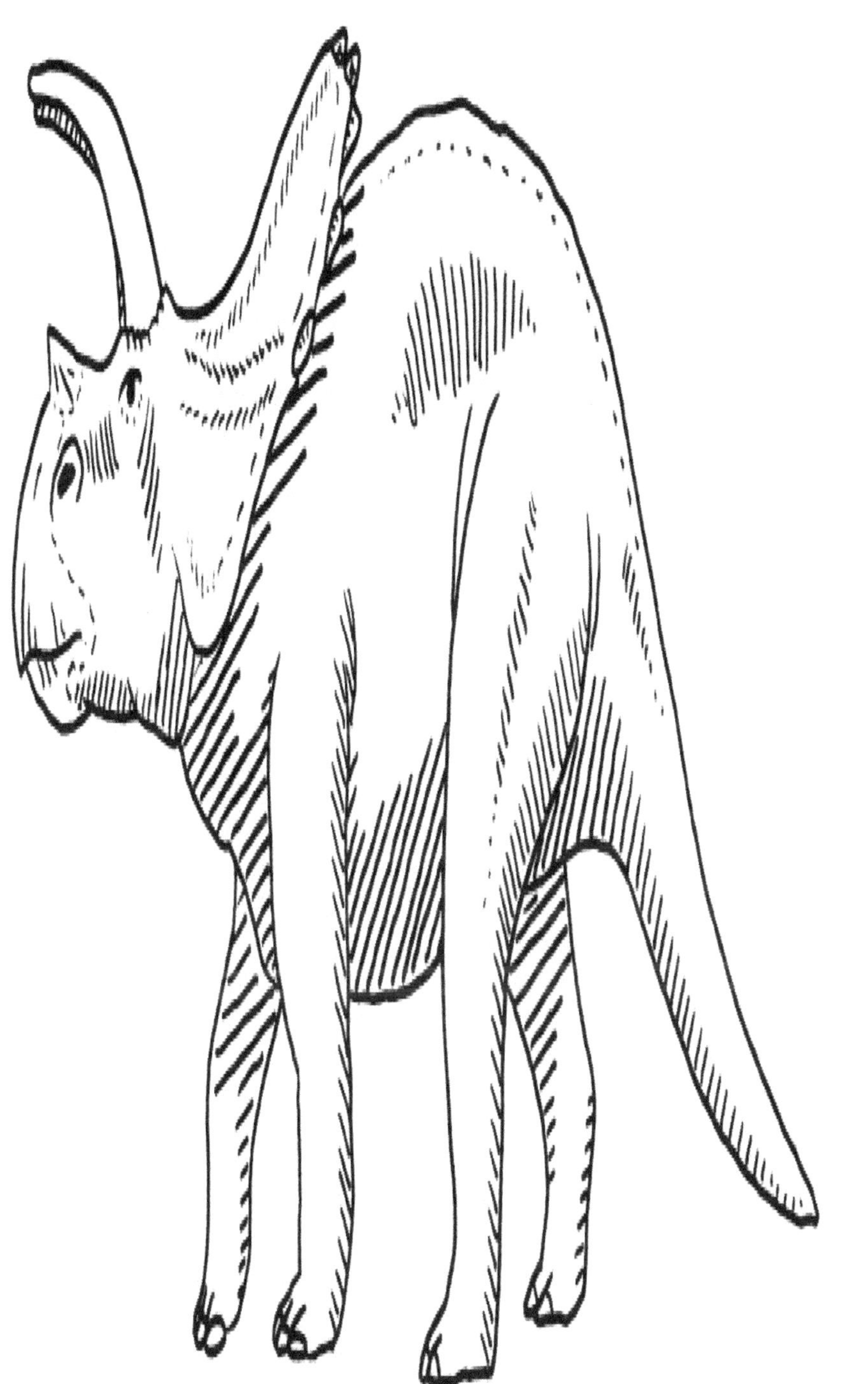

www.ingramcontent.com/pod-product-compliance
Lightning Source LLC
Chambersburg PA
CBHW061259140726
47998CB00006B/2295